D0063778

A First-Start Easy Reader

This easy reader contains only 60 different words,
repeated often to help the young reader develop
word recognition and interest in reading.

Basic word list for *Stop that Rabbit*

a	Mrs.	garden
she	Baker	beautiful
he	long	again
the	rose	stems
and	roses	leaves
to	big	Jane
but	next	lived
was	door	every
who	day	loves
did	very	loved
you	mad	smell
no	pick	touch
so	were	picked
I	said	never
are	that	watered
sat	why	someone
is	fed	rabbit
in	they	broken
had	stop	waited
one	bent	hungry

Stop That Rabbit

Written by Sharon Peters

Illustrated by Don Silverstein

Troll Associates

Mrs. Baker had a garden.

She had a beautiful rose garden.

The roses had long stems
and big leaves.

③

Jane lived next door.

Jane loved roses.

Jane loved to smell the roses.

She loved to touch the roses.

But Jane never picked the roses.

Mrs. Baker watered the roses.

9

One day, Mrs. Baker was very mad.

Someone picked the roses.

The roses were bent and broken.

"Jane, did you pick the roses?"

"No," said Jane.

"I never pick the roses."

"The roses are bent and broken,"

said Mrs. Baker.

Mrs. Baker sat and waited.

And Jane sat and waited.

"Stop!" said Jane.

"Stop that rabbit!"

''The rabbit is in the rose garden!''

"The rabbit is hungry," said Mrs. Baker.

"The rabbit loves the long stems and big leaves."

"That is why he picked the roses,"

said Mrs. Baker.

So Mrs. Baker and Jane fed the rabbit.

Every day they fed the rabbit.

And the rabbit never picked

the roses again!